Usborne
1001
Pirate
things to spot
Sticker Book

Rob Lloyd Jones
Illustrated and designed by Teri Gower

Additional design by Michelle Lawrence
Cover design by Nelupa Hussain
Edited by Anna Milbourne

Contents

Things to spot

These pirates are a lively bunch of scurvy sea dogs. They love fighting, partying and searching for buried treasure. Each scene in this book has all kinds of exciting pirate things for you to find and count. There are 1001 things to spot altogether.

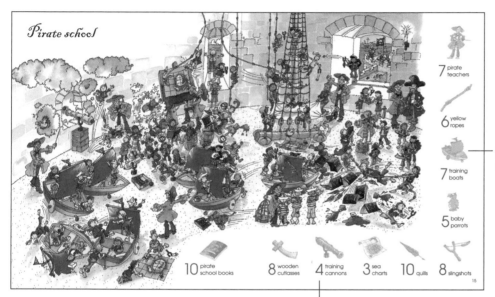

Pirate school

7 pirate teachers

6 yellow ropes

7 training boats

5 baby parrots

10 pirate school books

8 wooden cutlasses

4 training cannons

3 sea charts

10 quills

8 slingshots

15

Each little faded picture shows you what to look for in the big picture.

The number by each faded picture shows how many of that thing you need to find.

When you've found all of each thing, put a matching sticker on top of the faded picture. You'll find the stickers in the middle of the book.

This is Jack, the cabin boy on the pirate ship. He's always busy doing all the pirates' hard work. See if you can spot him in each scene, and then help him with his treasure hunt on page 30.

Life at sea

1 pirate captain

10 striped T-shirts

7 mops

4 telescopes

5 purple pirate hats

9 rats

7 sacks of grain

10 scrawny chickens

3 ship's cats

4

5 pirates on
the rigging

The captain's feast

10 ships in bottles **9** mice **7** bowls of stew **6** pineapples **8** chicken legs

 5 pirates with eye patches

9 lanterns

 10 cups of punch

 **5** fat cats

 **3** pirates in hammocks

Attack!

10 cutlasses

6 parrots shrieking

5 fist fights

10 flintlocks

8 blunderbusses

4 men walking the plank

7 tied-up prisoners

9 grappling hooks

8 cannons

9 cannonballs

Keeping shipshape

5 saws

10 spotted lizards

7 dice

4 pirates sewing sails

8 ladders

10 woodworms

5 buckets of tar

9 hammers

7 scrubbing brushes

3 campfires

Pirate port

 **9** pieces of eight

5 carthorses

 **9** baskets of fish

 5 parrots in cages

 **10** Jolly Rogers

12

 **3** pirates with peg legs  **6** anchors  **10** barrels of gunpowder   **8** stray dogs  **5** pelicans

Pirate school

10 pirate school books

7 pirate teachers

6 yellow ropes

7 training boats

5 baby parrots

8 wooden cutlasses

4 training cannons

3 sea charts

10 quills

8 slingshots

Pirate races

4 pirates water-skiing

10 seaweed pom-poms

4 pirates diving

10 pirate armbands

8 blue pairs of shorts

9 seagulls

2 surfboards

7 dolphins

1 finishing flag

16

Use these stickers on pages 4-5.

Use these stickers on pages 6-7.

Use these stickers on pages 8-9.

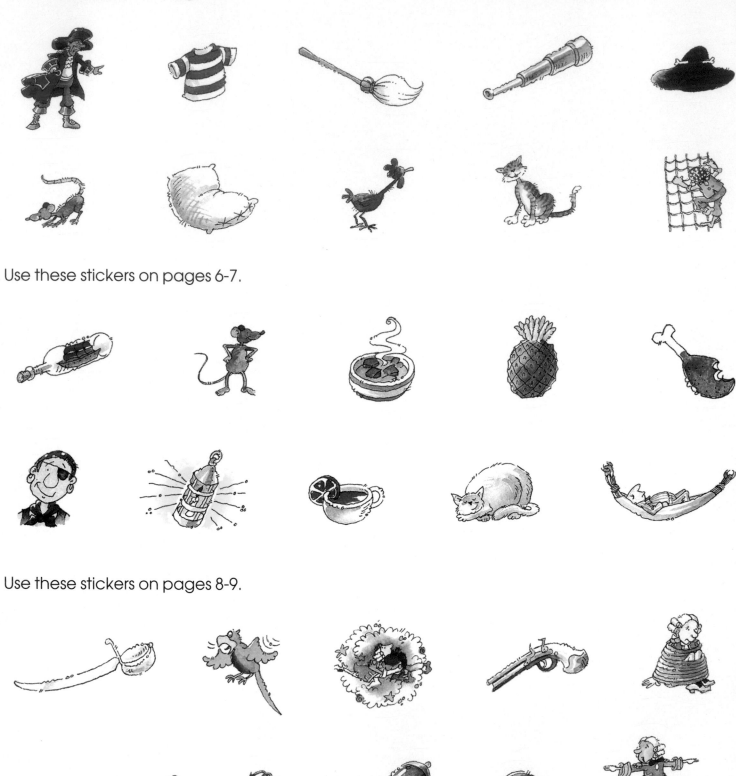

Use these stickers on pages 10-11.

Use these stickers on pages 12-13.

Use these stickers on pages 14-15.

Use these stickers on pages 16-17.

Use these stickers on pages 18-19.

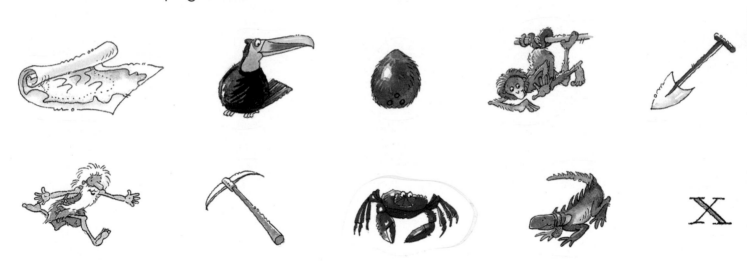

Use these stickers on pages 20-21.

Use these stickers on pages 22-23.

Use these stickers on pages 24-25.

Use these stickers on pages 26-27.

Use these stickers on pages 28-29.

Use these stickers on pages 30-31.

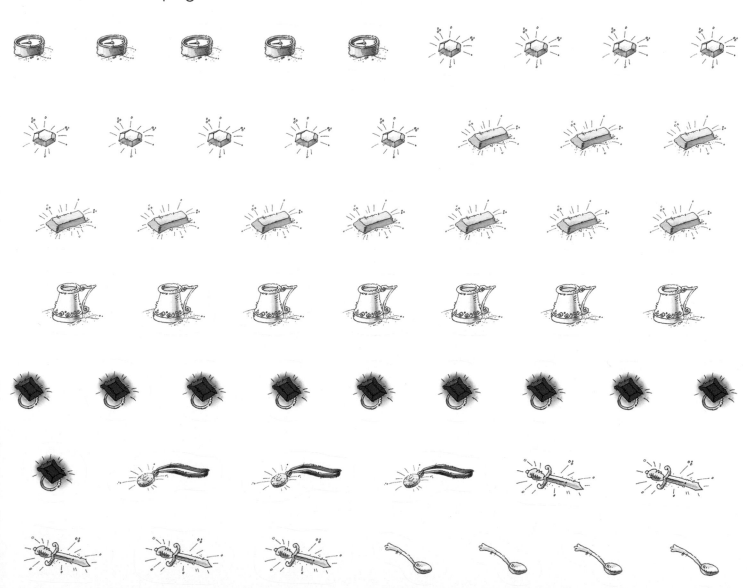

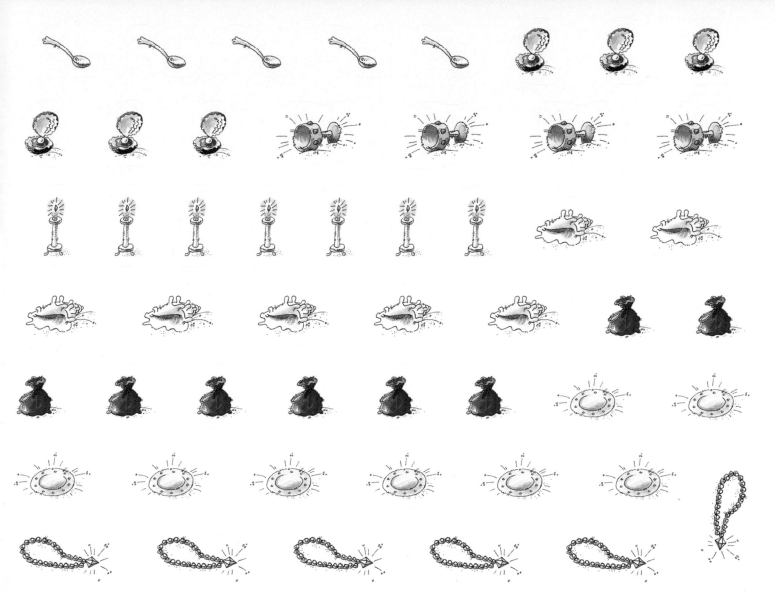

You could reward yourself by sticking one of these stickers on every page when you've found all the things around the edges.

6 turtles

Treasure island

4 treasure maps
6 toucans
8 coconuts
9 monkeys
10 shovels

2 castaways

7 pickaxes

9 crabs

10 iguanas

1 x-marks-the-spot

Pirate party

11 pirate party hats

4 barrels rolling

3 fiddles

9 flower garlands

5 monkeys dancing

9 plates of party cakes

7 chinese lanterns

6 drums

8 lollipops

10 pirate balloons

Monsters of the deep

 **7** tiger sharks

 **9** electric eels

 **1** smiling crocodile

 **10** spider crabs

 **5** frying pans

 **10** battle axes

 **6** barracudas

 **8** chickens flapping

 4 swordfish

22

10 sea
snakes

Ghost ship

9 skeleton pirates

4 mummies

9 pirate ghosts

5 pirates trembling

6 vultures

9 vampire bats

10 giant cobwebs

8 scary spiders

3 creepy coffins

6 vampire rats

Stormy sea

10 men overboard

5 buckets

4 bolts of lightning

8 life rings

5 pirate umbrellas

5 seasick pirates

8 shark fins

9 barrels floating

1 lighthouse

10 pirates in raincoats

Shipwreck

1 treasure chest

4 octopuses

7 broken cannons

6 rusty cutlasses

10 gold doubloons

 **9** mermaids **10** jellyfish **8** sea horses **5** messages in bottles **7** clownfish

Treasure hunt

Jack has found a wooden chest, full of treasure collected by the pirates on their adventures. Look back through the book to see if you can find it all, and add a sticker here for each thing you find.

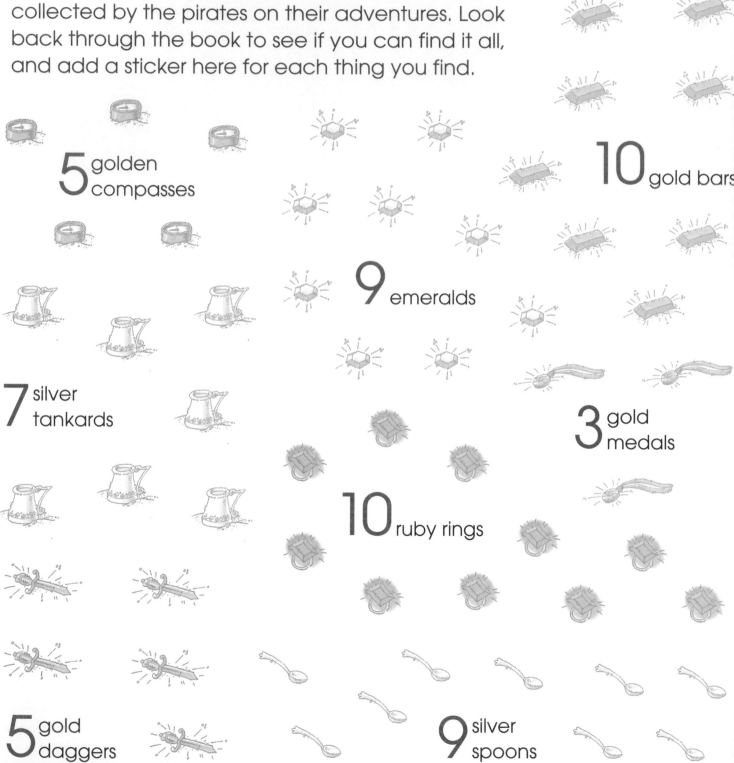

5 golden compasses

10 gold bars

9 emeralds

7 silver tankards

3 gold medals

10 ruby rings

5 gold daggers

9 silver spoons

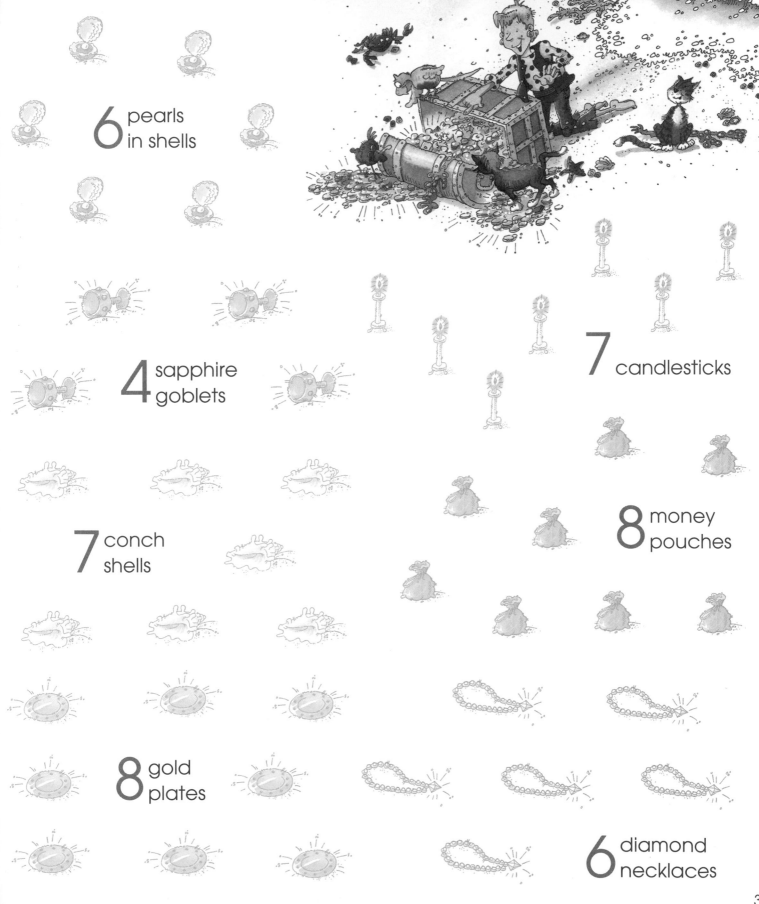

6 pearls in shells

4 sapphire goblets

7 conch shells

8 gold plates

7 candlesticks

8 money pouches

6 diamond necklaces

Answers

Did you spot all the treasure?
Here's where you can find it:

7 silver tankards:
The captain's feast
(pages 6-7)

9 silver spoons:
Pirate party
(pages 20-21)

7 candlesticks:
Ghost ship
(pages 24-25)

8 gold plates:
The captain's feast
(pages 6-7)

10 gold bars:
Keeping shipshape
(pages 10-11)

7 conch shells:
Treasure island
(pages 18-19)

6 diamond necklaces:
Shipwreck
(pages 28-29)

9 emeralds:
Stormy sea
(pages 26-27)

5 gold daggers:
Attack!
(pages 8-9)

5 golden compasses:
Pirate school
(pages 14-15)

4 sapphire goblets:
Life at sea
(pages 4-5)

3 gold medals:
Pirate races
(pages 16-17)

8 money pouches:
Pirate port
(pages 12-13)

6 pearls in shells:
Monsters of the deep
(pages 22-23)

10 ruby rings:
Shipwreck
(pages 28-29)

First published in 2014 by Usborne Publishing Ltd.,
Usborne House, 83-85 Saffron Hill, London EC1N 8RT, England. www.usborne.co.uk
Copyright © 2014, 2007, Usborne Publishing Ltd. The name Usborne and the devices ♀ ⊕ are Trade Marks of Usborne Publishing Ltd.
Printed in Heshan, Guangdong, China. U.E. First published in America 2014.